Comprehension Skills

Level 2
English

Welcome to ■SCHOLASTIC studySM▲RT !

Comprehension Skills provides opportunities for structured and repeated practice of specific reading skills at age-appropriate levels to help your child develop comprehension skills.

It is often a challenge to help a child develop the different types of reading skills, especially as she encounters an increasing variety of texts. The age-appropriate and engaging texts will encourage your child to read and sift out the important information essential to read specific kinds of texts. As your child progresses through the levels, she will encounter a greater variety of skills and texts while continuing to practice previously learnt skills at a more difficult level to ensure mastery.

Every section targets a specific reading skill and the repeated practice of the skill ensures your child masters the reading skill. There are extension activities that can be done for specific reading skills to encourage your child to delve even deeper into the texts.

How to use this book?

1. Introduce the target reading skill at the beginning of each section to your child.

2. Let your child complete the reading exercises.

3. Reinforce your child's learning with an extension activity at the end of each activity. These activities provide additional practice, and extend your child's learning of the particular reading skill.

Note: To avoid the awkward 'he or she' construction, the pronouns in this book will refer to the female gender.

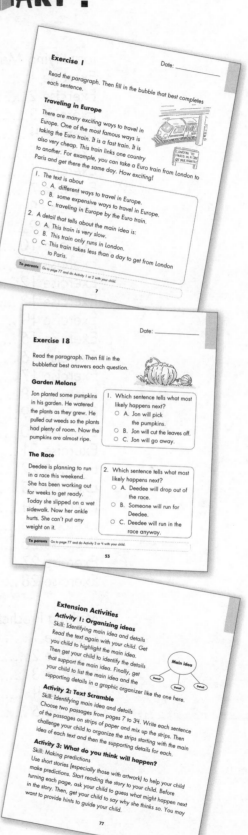

Contents

Identifying Main Ideas and Supporting Details

Reading comprehension involves numerous thinking skills. Identifying main ideas and the details that support them is one such skill. A reader who is adept at identifying main ideas makes better sense of a text and increases his or her comprehension of what is being communicated. The passages and questions in this section will help your child learn to recognize main ideas and the details that develop them.

Understanding the main idea of a passage is to be able to have a broad overall understanding of what a passage is all about. This section will provide opportunities for your child to understand that supporting details fill in information about the main idea and that the main idea is bigger and broader than the supporting details.

The extension activities provide additional challenges to your child to encourage and develop her understanding of the particular comprehension skill.

Exercise 1

Read the paragraph. Then fill in the bubble that best completes each sentence.

Traveling in Europe

There are many exciting ways to travel in
Europe. One of the most famous ways is
taking the Euro train. It is a fast train. It is
also very cheap. This train links one country
to another. For example, you can take a Euro train from London to
Paris and get there the same day. How exciting!

1. The text is about
   - ○ A. different ways to travel in Europe.
   - ○ B. some expensive ways to travel in Europe.
   - ○ C. traveling in Europe by the Euro train.

2. A detail that tells about the main idea is:
   - ○ A. This train is very slow.
   - ○ B. This train only runs in London.
   - ○ C. This train takes less than a day to get from London
     to Paris.

To parents Go to page 77 and do Activity 1 or 2 with your child.

Exercise 2

Read the paragraph. Then fill in the bubble that best completes each sentence.

Traveling Light

Backpacking is a cheap way to travel. When you go backpacking, you can only take one big knapsack. This way, you can move around very easily. Most backpackers live in youth hostels or cheap motels. This means they get to live cheaply in another country.

1. The text is about
    ○ A. living in motels.
    ○ B. living in youth hostels.
    ○ C. backpacking.

2. A detail that tells about the main idea is:
    ○ A. Backpackers live in hotels.
    ○ B. Backpackers live with friends.
    ○ C. Backpackers live in hostels.

To parents Go to page 77 and do Activity 1 or 2 with your child.

Exercise 3

Read the paragraph. Then fill in the bubble that best completes each sentence.

Fire-fighters

Fire-fighters have a noble job. They save lives in danger. They also put fires out. They wear heavy uniforms with protective gloves and boots. They also carry an oxygen tank with them. Their fire gear protects them from the hot fire. Maybe I should become a fire-fighter when I grow up.

1. The text is about
   - ○ A. oxygen tanks.
   - ○ B. the work of a fire-fighter.
   - ○ C. fighting fires.

2. A detail that tells about the main idea is:
   - ○ A. A fire-fighter wears fire protective gear.
   - ○ B. A fire-fighter's uniform is light.
   - ○ C. A fire-fighter carries a carbon dioxide tank.

To parents Go to page 77 and do Activity 1 or 2 with your child.

Exercise 4

Read the paragraph. Then fill in the bubble that best completes each sentence.

Being Ill is No Fun!

Linda was ill in the hospital. She had dengue fever. Her temperature was very high. She had a terrible headache. She also felt very miserable and lonely being stuck at the hospital. She wished she was at home. She longed to play with her younger brothers and her beautiful kittens.

1. The text is about
   ○ A. Linda being unhappy.
   ○ B. Linda missing her brothers.
   ○ C. Linda being ill at the hospital.

2. A detail that tells about the main idea is:
   ○ A. Linda had a pounding headache.
   ○ B. Linda was happy to be left alone.
   ○ C. Linda wanted to play with her friends.

To parents Go to page 77 and do Activity 1 or 2 with your child.

10

Exercise 5

Read the paragraph. Then fill in the bubble that best completes each sentence.

Birthdays

Birthdays are important days to remember. They mark the day a person is born. People in many countries celebrate birthdays. They celebrate them with a gift, party or even kind actions. By remembering and celebrating someone's birthday, we show that person how important he or she is.

1. The text is about
    - ○ A. important days.
    - ○ B. the importance of birthdays.
    - ○ C. birthday parties.

2. A detail that tells about the main idea is:
    - ○ A. Birthdays are celebrated in all countries.
    - ○ B. Birthdays are celebrated with gifts.
    - ○ C. Birthdays are celebrated for important people only.

To parents Go to page 77 and do Activity 1 or 2 with your child.

Date: _____

Exercise 6

Read the paragraph. Then fill in the bubble that best completes each sentence.

Soap Operas

My mother and aunties love to watch soap operas. Their favorite soap opera is called 'The Bold and The Beautiful'. They watch this every evening. They will not miss this soap opera for anything. I can't watch my cartoons on television when they are watching their soap opera.

1. The text is about
    ○ A. the writer's mother and aunties.
    ○ B. watching television.
    ○ C. watching soap operas.

2. A detail that tells about the main idea is:
    ○ A. Their favorite soap opera is 'Falcon Crest'.
    ○ B. They watch soap operas every morning.
    ○ C. They always watch their favorite soap opera.

To parents Go to page 77 and do Activity 1 or 2 with your child.

Date: _____

Exercise 7

Read the paragraph. Then fill in the bubble that best completes each sentence.

Water

Drinking lots of water is good for you. You should drink at least six cups of water a day. This will make sure you do not have any toxins in your body. You can either drink the water cold or warm. It does not matter. What is important is that you drink it every day.

1. The text is about
   - ○ A. drinking enough water.
   - ○ B. drinking warm or cold water.
   - ○ C. water in your body.

2. A detail that tells about the main idea is:
   - ○ A. You should drink at least six cups of water a day.
   - ○ B. You should drink at least three cups of water a day.
   - ○ C. You should not drink water every day.

To parents   Go to page 77 and do Activity 1 or 2 with your child.

Exercise 8

Read the paragraph. Then fill in the bubble that best completes each sentence.

My First Ball

I am going for my first ball at school tomorrow. I am looking forward to it. My teacher says there will be lots of food and dancing. She has hired a very good deejay. He will play very good music. We will all have to dance at the ball. This means I will have to learn how to dance first.

1. The text is about
   - ○ A. a red ball.
   - ○ B. a ball at school.
   - ○ C. dance class.

2. A detail that tells about the main idea is:
   - ○ A. There will be lots of drinks at the ball.
   - ○ B. There will be a sound machine at the ball.
   - ○ C. There will be a deejay at the ball.

To parents Go to page 77 and do Activity 1 or 2 with your child.

Exercise 9

Read the paragraph. Then fill in the bubble that best completes each sentence.

Weddings

Weddings are wonderful. A wedding is very special for the man and woman getting married. It is a time when they can celebrate their love for each other. Families get together at weddings too. There you get to see the different family members you have. Maybe you'll see your hilarious Uncle Bill or your funny Aunt Nancy!

1. The text is about
   ○ A. the joy of weddings.
   ○ B. funny uncles and aunties.
   ○ C. love.

2. A detail that tells about the main idea is:
   ○ A. Weddings are funny events.
   ○ B. Weddings are a time when families get together.
   ○ C. Weddings are for married people only.

To parents Go to page 77 and do Activity 1 or 2 with your child.

Exercise 10

Read the paragraph. Then fill in the bubble that best completes each sentence.

Home For Animals

Zoos are places that keep different kinds of animals. They are home to many animals. Zoos must be kept clean all the time. This ensures that the animals have a good environment to live in. Zoos are places where parents take their children. Children can learn about animals there.

1. The text is about
   - ○ A. different animals.
   - ○ B. keeping animals clean.
   - ○ C. zoos.

2. A detail that tells about the main idea is:
   - ○ A. Parents take their children to zoos.
   - ○ B. Zoos do not need to be cleaned.
   - ○ C. Children are not allowed at zoos.

To parents Go to page 77 and do Activity 1 or 2 with your child.

Exercise 11

Read the paragraph. Then fill in the bubble that best completes each sentence.

Love of Baseball

Baseball is a fun sport. Many people love to play baseball. Others love to watch it. Some favorite teams are the Red Soxs or the Yankees. Some people follow the game religiously. They do not miss a game no matter what the reason. They are die-hard fans!

1. The text is about
   - ○ A. baseball.
   - ○ B. fans.
   - ○ C. the Yankees.

2. A detail that tells about the main idea is:
   - ○ A. Many people love playing baseball.
   - ○ B. Their favorite teams are the Red Bulls and the Yankees.
   - ○ C. People do not like to watch baseball.

To parents Go to page 77 and do Activity 1 or 2 with your child.

Exercise 12

Read the paragraph. Then fill in the bubble that best completes each sentence.

Speed

Some people like driving fast cars. They enjoy driving at high speed. They love the feel of the wind blowing through their hair. When I grow up, I want to drive a fast car. The car I would like to drive is a Ferrari. It looks nice and has a powerful engine.

1. The text is about
   - ○ A. fast cars.
   - ○ B. Ferraris.
   - ○ C. cars.

2. A detail that tells about the main idea is:
   - ○ A. The wind blowing through your hair is a great feeling.
   - ○ B. Cars can go faster when the wind is blowing.
   - ○ C. The writer would like to ride a motorcycle.

To parents Go to page 77 and do Activity 1 or 2 with your child.

Date: _____

Exercise 13

Read the paragraph. Then fill in the bubble that best completes each sentence.

The Visually Impaired

The visually impaired need our help. This is because they are unable to see. When we see a visually impaired person we should be ready to offer help. If you see a visually impaired person crossing the road, you could offer to hold their arm and take them to the other side of the road.

1. The text is about
    ○ A. helping the visually impaired.
    ○ B. crossing the road.
    ○ C. holding hands.

2. A detail that tells about the main idea is:
    ○ A. We should help the visually impaired cross the road.
    ○ B. We should walk behind the visually impaired when crossing the road.
    ○ C. We should run away from the visually impaired.

To parents   Go to page 77 and do Activity 1 or 2 with your child.

Exercise 14

Read the paragraph. Then fill in the bubble that best completes each sentence.

Fitness First

Individual fitness is very important. A good fitness level ensures good health. To build your fitness you must exercise at least three times a week for half an hour. Play outdoors in the park or take up an active sport. You must also eat good and nutritious food to build your fitness level.

1. The text is about
   - ○ A. the importance of playing games.
   - ○ B. the importance of eating well.
   - ○ C. the importance of being fit.

2. A detail that tells about the main idea is:
   - ○ A. You should exercise five times a week for half an hour.
   - ○ B. You should exercise three times a week for an hour.
   - ○ C. You should exercise three times a week for half an hour.

To parents   Go to page 77 and do Activity 1 or 2 with your child.

Exercise 15

Read the paragraph. Then fill in the bubble that best completes each sentence.

Pets

Pets are animals that are kept at home. People keep pets at home to keep them company. Pets also bring enjoyment. They often entertain their owners by their funny tricks. If you have a pet, you must take good care of your pet. Feed it regularly and keep it clean and healthy.

1. The text is about
   - ○ A. keeping pets.
   - ○ B. keeping company.
   - ○ C. keeping clean and healthy.

2. A detail that tells about the main idea is:
   - ○ A. Pets keep people company.
   - ○ B. Pets are annoying.
   - ○ C. Keeping pets is a waste of time.

To parents   Go to page 77 and do Activity 1 or 2 with your child.

Exercise 16

Read the paragraph. Then fill in the bubble that best completes each sentence.

A Crown of Rubies

My name is Alice. I have always wanted to be a princess. I would like to wear a crown with rubies on my head. Every morning I pretend to be a princess. I put on the plastic tiara my mother bought for me. I imagine myself to be a royal princess with a beautiful carriage.

1. The text is about
   - ○ A. Alice's dream of being a princess.
   - ○ B. princesses and tiaras.
   - ○ C. rubies on a crown.

2. A detail that tells about the main idea is:
   - ○ A. Every morning Alice wears a plastic tiara.
   - ○ B. Every morning Alice wears a set of earrings.
   - ○ C. Every morning Alice wears a new gown.

To parents   Go to page 77 and do Activity 1 or 2 with your child.

Exercise 17

Read the paragraph. Then fill in the bubble that best completes each sentence.

An Orange a Day Keeps the Doctor Away

Oranges are very good for health. They have natural Vitamin C. Vitamin C helps to make us strong so we don't fall sick easily. It is also good for our skin. There are many different types of oranges. The most common orange is called the Valencia orange. Doctors advise that one should take an orange a day to keep healthy.

1. The text is about
   ○ A. oranges.
   ○ B. Vitamin C.
   ○ C. fruits.

2. A detail that tells about the main idea is:
   ○ A. You should have two oranges a day.
   ○ B. You should have an orange a day.
   ○ C. You should have an orange every other day.

To parents Go to page 77 and do Activity 1 or 2 with your child.

23

Exercise 18

Read the paragraph. Then fill in the bubble that best completes each sentence.

Diana

Princess Diana was the princess of Wales. She belonged to the British Royal family. She was a very beautiful woman. She had two sons. Their names are Prince William and Prince Harry. She loved her sons very much. She was also known as 'the people's princess'.

1. The text is about
   - ○ A. Princess Diana.
   - ○ B. Prince William.
   - ○ C. Queen Diana.

2. A detail that tells about the main idea is:
   - ○ A. Princess Diana's children were William and Kate.
   - ○ B. Princess Diana's children were William and Harry.
   - ○ C. Princess Diana was known as 'the people's queen'.

To parents   Go to page 77 and do Activity 1 or 2 with your child.

24

Exercise 19

Read the paragraph. Then fill in the bubble that best completes each sentence.

Feeling Sleepy

Samuel had a very heavy lunch today. He had three pieces of chicken, with vegetables and rice. He felt very full. He wasn't able to perform well for sports practice. His teacher was very disappointed with him and scolded him. Samuel was saddened by this.

1. The text is about
   - ○ A. Samuel's heavy lunch.
   - ○ B. having lunch.
   - ○ C. vegetables and rice.

2. A detail that tells about the main idea is:
   - ○ A. After a heavy lunch, Samuel did not do well at sports.
   - ○ B. After a heavy lunch, Samuel did well at sports.
   - ○ C. Samuel's teacher was happy with his performance.

To parents   Go to page 77 and do Activity 1 or 2 with your child.

25

Exercise 20

Read the paragraph. Then fill in the bubble that best completes each sentence.

Jigsaw Puzzles

Jigsaw puzzles are fun to do. They come in different shapes and sizes. Jigsaw puzzles come with interesting pictures and colors. This includes pictures of nature, buildings, castles and mountains. When you are trying to fit the pieces together, you can look at the picture on the box. This will help you finish the puzzle.

1. The text is about
    ○ A. buildings and castles.
    ○ B. enjoying a jigsaw puzzle.
    ○ C. shapes and sizes.

2. A detail that tells about the main idea is:
    ○ A. Jigsaw puzzles come in different shapes and sizes.
    ○ B. Jigsaw puzzles all have the same shapes and sizes.
    ○ C. Jigsaw puzzles come with ugly pictures.

To parents Go to page 77 and do Activity 1 or 2 with your child.

Exercise 21

Read the paragraph. Then fill in the bubble that best completes each sentence.

Read for Knowledge

Children's encyclopedias are important books to have for children. These encyclopedias contain different types of knowledge. They tell children things they need to know from different parts of  the world. They tell about how things work. Every child should make the effort to use encyclopedias.

1. The text is about
   - ○ A. the importance of encyclopedias for children.
   - ○ B. the importance of studying.
   - ○ C. the importance of books.

2. A detail that tells about the main idea is:
   - ○ A. Encyclopedias contain different types of knowledge.
   - ○ B. Children should not read encyclopedias.
   - ○ C. Encyclopedias are very expensive.

To parents Go to page 77 and do Activity 1 or 2 with your child.

Exercise 22

Read the paragraph. Then fill in the bubble that best completes each sentence.

Running in the Family

Josephine's father is a famous runner. He represents his country in international competitions. Her brother also runs very well. He runs for his school and the state. Josephine has just started running for the track team in her school. She hopes she will do as well as her father and brother.

1. The text is about
   ○ A. how Josephine's family is good in running.
   ○ B. international running competitions.
   ○ C. good runners.

2. A detail that tells about the main idea is:
   ○ A. Josephine's father does not run.
   ○ B. Josephine has just joined the track team.
   ○ C. Josephine's sister is a good runner.

To parents Go to page 77 and do Activity 1 or 2 with your child.

Exercise 23

Read the paragraph. Then fill in the bubble that best completes each sentence.

Breakfast Around the World

Americans like toast, eggs, and cereal. In China people eat congee, a thick rice. People in Japan often have a soup called miso. Pancakes made from lentil beans are favored in India. Bread and coffee with milk are the most popular breakfast foods in France. Breakfast around the world is a matter of different tastes.

1. The text is about
   - ○ A. people in China and Japan liking different foods.
   - ○ B. cereal being a popular breakfast food in America.
   - ○ C. the different foods people eat for breakfast around the world.

2. A detail that tells about the main idea is:
   - ○ A. Breakfast is an important meal.
   - ○ B. Everyone eats eggs at breakfast.
   - ○ C. People in India eat lentil pancakes.

To parents Go to page 77 and do Activity 1 or 2 with your child.

Date: _____

Exercise 24

Read the paragraph. Then fill in the bubble that best completes each sentence.

Helpful Horses

Horses are often helpers for humans. In some communities the police ride horses to control large crowds. Cowboys use horses to help round up herds of cattle. In some countries farmers still use horses to pull plows or wagons. People also use horses to carry them from place to place.

1. The text is about
   - ○ A. the different jobs that horses can do.
   - ○ B. how the police use horses in crowds.
   - ○ C. the ways that animals help people.

2. A detail that tells more about the main idea is:
   - ○ A. Cowboys use horses in their work.
   - ○ B. The kinds of horses used in police work
   - ○ C. The names of countries using farm horses

To parents   Go to page 77 and do Activity 1 or 2 with your child.

Exercise 25

Read the paragraph. Then fill in the bubble that best completes each sentence.

Trucks at Airports

It takes a lot of trucks to get an airplane ready to fly. Fuel trucks are very important. They fill the fuel tanks of planes. Baggage trucks carry people's suitcases to and from planes. Still other trucks deliver food. You might also see mail trucks and cargo trucks. Also standing by at airports are repair trucks.

1. The text is about
   - ○ A. how airplanes are like trucks.
   - ○ B. how some trucks carry food.
   - ○ C. how trucks help planes.

2. A detail that tells about the main idea is:
   - ○ A. Trucks are more important than planes.
   - ○ B. Many people carry on their luggage.
   - ○ C. Airplanes depend on trucks for fuel.

To parents   Go to page 77 and do Activity 1 or 2 with your child.

Date: _____

Exercise 26

Read the paragraph. Then fill in the bubble that best completes each sentence.

Remembering Stories Long Ago

The earliest people did not have a written language. Instead, people learned things by telling and listening to stories. How did storytellers recall everything? Some drew pictures on cave walls. Some made up chants to the rhythm of drums. Other storytellers made belts or necklaces. Colored threads, beads and special knots stood for different events.

1. The text is about
    - ○ A. drawings on cave walls long ago.
    - ○ B. why there were no books or magazines.
    - ○ C. the different ways storytellers recalled events.

2. A detail that tells more about the main idea is:
    - ○ A. Which people became storytellers
    - ○ B. Beads on belts helped recall things.
    - ○ C. What kinds of stories people told

To parents   Go to page 77 and do Activity 1 or 2 with your child.

32

Exercise 27

Read the paragraph. Then fill in the bubble that best completes each sentence.

Looking at Nylon

Nylon is a kind of plastic. Like other plastics, nylon is made from crude oil. One of the most important uses of nylon is in making clothing. You may be wearing something made of nylon today. Nylon is also used to make carpets. Where else will you see nylon? It's used in fishing nets and in the small wheels found in gears. A tennis racquet also has nylon strings.

1. The text is about
   - ○ A. nylon.
   - ○ B. carpets made from nylon.
   - ○ C. the different uses of plastic.

2. A detail that tells more about the main idea is:
   - ○ A. Nylon is used for tennis racquet strings.
   - ○ B. Rayon is also a man-made fabric.
   - ○ C. Racquet frames were once made of wood.

To parents Go to page 77 and do Activity 1 or 2 with your child.

Exercise 28

Read the paragraph. Then fill in the bubble that best completes each sentence.

Happy Birthday, Authors

March is a good month to celebrate authors' birthdays. You can begin on March 2. That's the day when Dr Seuss was born in 1904. March 11 is the birth date of Ezra Jack Keats. Have you ever read his book *The Snowy Day*? On March 12 you can celebrate the birthday of Virginia Hamilton. One of her well-known books is *The People Could Fly: American Black Folktales*.

1. The text is about
   - ○ A. authors with March birthdays.
   - ○ B. the birthday of Virginia Hamilton.
   - ○ C. favorite children's book authors.

2. A detail that tells more about the main idea is:
   - ○ A. How Dr Seuss got started writing
   - ○ B. Ways to celebrate an author's birthday
   - ○ C. Ezra Jack Keats was born on March 11.

To parents   Go to page 77 and do Activity 1 or 2 with your child.

Making Predictions

Making predictions is one of the many essential reading skills that young readers need to have. A reader who can think ahead to determine what may happen next or how an event may turn out gains a richer understanding of a text. The passages and questions in this section will help your child learn to make reasonable predictions and anticipate probabilities.

This section will provide opportunities for your child to guess what is likely to happen based on information that she already knows as well as the information in the text.

The extension activities provide additional challenges to your child to encourage and develop her understanding of the particular comprehension skill.

Exercise 1

Read the paragraph. Then fill in the bubble that best answers each question.

Biking in a New Place

Tourists like to rent bikes to explore the city. Tourists often forget they are not familiar with the area. They almost never take notes on all the turns they make.

1. Which sentence tells what most likely happens next?
   - ○ A. Tourists will fall off their bikes.
   - ○ B. Tourists will get lost.
   - ○ C. Tourists will stop exploring.

Wonderful Fruits

Fruits are delicious. However, you must be careful not to buy unripe fruits. An unripe fruit's skin will be hard. If you are not careful, you may be eating an unripe fruit without knowing it.

2. Which sentence tells what most likely happens next?
   - ○ A. It will make you happy.
   - ○ B. It will give you a stomachache.
   - ○ C. It will make you strong.

To parents   Go to page 77 and do Activity 3 or 4 with your child.

36

Exercise 2

Read the paragraph. Then fill in the bubble that best answers each question.

Cleaning up after Ourselves

Cleaning up after ourselves is a good habit. When we eat something we need to wash our plates. We also have to wipe the table so it remains clean. If we do not do this, we will leave a dirty mess.

1. Which sentence tells what most likely happens next?
   ○ A. The mess will attract ants and flies.
   ○ B. The mess will attract bees.
   ○ C. The mess will attract snails.

Playing Darts

Playing darts can be dangerous. Darts have very sharp ends. You should never stand under the dart board when a game is on. If the player misses the board, the dart can fall to the floor.

2. Which sentence tells what most likely happens next?
   ○ A. The dart may hurt you.
   ○ B. The dart will miss you.
   ○ C. The dart will be bent.

To parents Go to page 77 and do Activity 3 or 4 with your child.

Exercise 3

Read the paragraph. Then fill in the bubble that best answers each question.

A Full Nappy

Baby Sam has been crying for the past half hour. His mother does not know what is wrong with him. When she finally picks him up, she realizes he has a full, wet nappy. He has also dirtied his clothes.

1. Which sentence tells what most likely happens next?
   - ○ A. Baby Sam will fall asleep.
   - ○ B. Baby Sam will laugh.
   - ○ C. Baby Sam's mother will change his nappy.

Oh No! Electricity!

Ellie was using her computer. Her nephew, Alex, accidentally touched the computer plug. He shouted in shock and pain when he felt it. Ellie got up very quickly to help him.

2. Which sentence tells what most likely happens next?
   - ○ A. Ellie will scold Alex.
   - ○ B. Ellie will take Alex to the doctor.
   - ○ C. Ellie will laugh at Alex.

To parents Go to page 77 and do Activity 3 or 4 with your child.

Date: _____

Exercise 4

Read the paragraph. Then fill in the bubble that best answers each question.

Watching Hi-5

Sue loves watching Hi-5 every morning on television. It is a kids' musical show. This morning however, the television does not work. There is no electricity. Poor Sue!

1. Which sentence tells what most likely happens next?
   - ○ A. Sue will fall asleep.
   - ○ B. Sue will feel sad.
   - ○ C. Sue will start singing.

A Flat Battery

Eric forgot to charge his cell phone last night. The battery was flat. He needed to call the bank to make some payments. Then he needed to call the dentist because his tooth was aching. Eric had a busy day ahead.

2. Which sentence tells what most likely happens next?
   - ○ A. Eric will charge his phone battery.
   - ○ B. Eric will buy a new phone.
   - ○ C. Eric will throw away his phone.

To parents Go to page 77 and do Activity 3 or 4 with your child.

39

Date: _____

Exercise 5

Read the paragraph. Then fill in the bubble that best answers each question.

Leaving on a Jet Plane

Leaving for a holiday is always exciting. However, it can be stressful getting to the airport on time. For an international flight, you will have to be at the airport two hours before your flight. Some people get there only an hour and a half before their flight.

1. Which sentence tells what most likely happens next?
   - ○ A. They will have to rush.
   - ○ B. They will be angry.
   - ○ C. They will miss their flight.

Running a Mile

Jeff is all ready to run a mile for the first time. He is careful to follow the rules and warms up before he starts to run. But oh no! Jeff is not wearing proper running shoes.

2. Which sentence tells what most likely happens next?
   - ○ A. Jeff will hurt his feet.
   - ○ B. Jeff will run faster.
   - ○ C. Jeff will not feel tired.

To parents Go to page 77 and do Activity 3 or 4 with your child.

40

Date: _____

Exercise 6

Read the paragraph. Then fill in the bubble that best answers each question.

A Hospital Visit

This is Anne's first visit to the hospital. She is here to visit Grandma. Grandma just had an operation. When Anne walks into the hospital room, she sees her on the bed. Grandma looks very pale.

1. Which sentence tells what most likely happens next?
   - ○ A. Anne will start laughing.
   - ○ B. Anne will start crying.
   - ○ C. Anne will eat her grandmother's food.

A Wet Wall

Jim visits Alex often. They either play in Alex's house or at Finley Park. Today, Jim was waiting for Alex outside his house. He did not know he was leaning against a newly painted wall.

2. Which sentence tells what most likely happens next?
   - ○ A. Jim will repaint the wall.
   - ○ B. Jim will have paint on his clothes.
   - ○ C. Jim will start sneezing.

To parents Go to page 77 and do Activity 3 or 4 with your child.

Exercise 7

Read the paragraph. Then fill in the bubble that best answers each question.

First Time Away from Home

This is Carol's first time away from home. She has left home to study in Australia. She realizes she will not be able to see her family for a very long time. She feels very lonely as she lies on her bed.

1. Which sentence tells what most likely happens next?
   - ○ A. Carol will feel sad.
   - ○ B. Carol will feel angry.
   - ○ C. Carol will feel excited.

All Work and No Play

"All work and no play makes Jack a dull boy". This saying tells us that we must have a balance in whatever we do. We should always work hard. However, we also need time to relax. Some people work too hard!

2. Which sentence tells what most likely happens next?
   - ○ A. They will not have money.
   - ○ B. They will feel tired.
   - ○ C. They will not be successful.

To parents   Go to page 77 and do Activity 3 or 4 with your child.

Exercise 8

Read the paragraph. Then fill in the bubble that best answers each question.

Longing for Spicy Curry

Jacob has a terrible flu. He is constantly sneezing and he has a terrible sore throat. Jacob is longing to eat spicy curry. His mother says it is not good for his throat. He needs to eat something warm and soothing.

1. Which sentence tells what most likely happens next?
   ○ A. Jacob's mother will give him spicy curry.
   ○ B. Jacob's mother will give him fried chicken.
   ○ C. Jacob's mother will give him chicken soup.

Music Class

Lynn was attending her first music class. There, her teacher taught her how to sing and play the piano. Suddenly, while Lynn was playing the electric piano, the electricity went off.

2. Which sentence tells what most likely happens next?
   ○ A. Lynn will continue to play the electric piano.
   ○ B. Lynn will start to dance.
   ○ C. Lynn's class will end early.

To parents Go to page 77 and do Activity 3 or 4 with your child.

Date: _____

Exercise 9

Read the paragraph. Then fill in the bubble that best answers each question.

Out of Fuel

Dad has been driving around the whole day. He did not realize he was low on fuel. He did not see the fuel gauge light blinking many times. Suddenly, he felt the car start to jerk.

1. Which sentence tells what most likely happens next?
   - ○ A. The car will smoke up.
   - ○ B. The car will stop moving.
   - ○ C. The car will keep jerking.

A Low Battery

Vera had an important essay to write. She was planning to complete it at the café but she forgot to bring the charger for her laptop. The battery was low.

2. Which sentence tells what most likely happens next?
   - ○ A. Vera will buy a new computer.
   - ○ B. Vera will buy a new battery.
   - ○ C. Vera will write her assignment.

To parents   Go to page 77 and do Activity 3 or 4 with your child.

Exercise 10

Read the paragraph. Then fill in the bubble that best answers each question.

Setting the Alarm

Joe had something important to do in the morning. He set his alarm clock so that he would have enough time to get ready and be on time. However, the power got cut off in the night.

1. Which sentence tells what most likely happens next?
   - ○ A. Joe will be up early.
   - ○ B. Joe will get up late.
   - ○ C. Joe's alarm will go off as set.

Friendship Bands

Friendship bands show how important a friendship is to us. They come in pretty colors and patterns. We give friendship bands to close friends. Sometimes, we may forget to give a close friend a friendship band.

2. Which sentence tells what most likely happens next?
   - ○ A. Our friend will be happy.
   - ○ B. Our friend will be hurt.
   - ○ C. Our friend will not notice.

To parents Go to page 77 and do Activity 3 or 4 with your child.

Date: _____

Exercise 11

Read the paragraph. Then fill in the bubble that best answers each question.

Fried Chicken

It takes a lot of work to prepare fried chicken. First you have to prepare the flour batter. Then, heat the oil in the frying pan. Once this is done, you can place the chicken into the hot oil.

1. Which sentence tells what most likely happens next?
   ○ A. You will get hurt.
   ○ B. The chicken will be deep fried in the oil.
   ○ C. The chicken will break into pieces.

Busy People

Baby Vernon always refuses to eat his food. The only way you can get him to eat his meal is if you play 'Busy People' on television. Today his mother could not find the disk. Oh no!!

1. Which sentence tells what most likely happens next?
   ○ A. Vernon will eat his meal with no trouble.
   ○ B. Vernon will not eat his meal.
   ○ C. Vernon will watch another show.

To parents Go to page 77 and do Activity 3 or 4 with your child.

Exercise 12

Read the paragraph. Then fill in the bubble that best answers each question.

Baking Bread

Fred is making bread. He is adding yeast to make the bread rise. He was warned not to put too much yeast in his bread dough. Fred was not paying attention. He accidentally added extra yeast. What a disaster!

1. Which sentence tells what most likely happens next?
   - ○ A. The bread will rise too much.
   - ○ B. The bread will not rise.
   - ○ C. The bread will burn.

A Water Problem

Tara's sink keeps on leaking. There is water everywhere. Every time she mops up the water, a new puddle appears. Tara is very upset. She really needs help to solve her water problem.

2. Which sentence tells what most likely happens next?
   - ○ A. Tara will call a plumber.
   - ○ B. Tara will call a mechanic.
   - ○ C. Tara will call a doctor.

To parents   Go to page 77 and do Activity 3 or 4 with your child.

Exercise 13

Read the paragraph. Then fill in the bubble that best answers each question.

A Trip to the Fruit Mart

Molly wanted to buy some fruits at the fruit mart. She took a paper bag with her to the fruit mart. She did not realize there was a hole in the bag. As Molly put the fruits in the bag, her bag did not get heavier.

1. Which sentence tells what most likely happens next?
   - ○ A. Molly will go home with a bag of fruits.
   - ○ B. Molly will go home with a bag of vegetables.
   - ○ C. Molly's fruits will fall out from her bag.

Dressing Up

When attending a ballroom dinner, you will have to follow a dress code. You are not allowed to wear shorts and slippers. Sometimes, guests do not follow the dress code.

2. Which sentence tells what most likely happens next?
   - ○ A. They will be asked to leave.
   - ○ B. They will be invited in.
   - ○ C. They will be shouted at.

To parents Go to page 77 and do Activity 3 or 4 with your child.

Date: _____

Exercise 14

Read the paragraph. Then fill in the bubble that best answers each question.

Kelly's New Game

Kelly's mother bought her a new game. She loved it! She took it on the bus and showed it off to her friends. She then put the game down on the seat, and started talking with Paul. Soon, it was time to get off the bus.

1. Which sentence tells what most likely happens next?
   - ○ A. Kelly will lend Paul the game.
   - ○ B. Kelly will forget to take her game with her.
   - ○ C. Kelly will sell Paul the game.

A Happy Camper

Pete was camping in the woods. He quickly set up his tent. Then he collected some wood to make a campfire. It was time to cook the food he brought. Then he realized he had left the pan at home!

2. Which sentence tells what most likely happens next?
   - ○ A. Pete will not be able to cook.
   - ○ B. Pete's tent will catch fire.
   - ○ C. Pete will attract animals.

To parents Go to page 77 and do Activity 3 or 4 with your child.

Exercise 15

Read the paragraph. Then fill in the bubble that best answers each question.

A California Story

California is the raisin capital of the world. Farmers there begin by growing grapes. When the grapes are ripe, they are laid out in the dry, sunny air. The grapes begin to wrinkle as they lose their water. They change color, too.

1. Which sentence tells what most likely happens next?
   - ○ A. The grapes get rotten.
   - ○ B. Farmers water the grapes.
   - ○ C. The grapes turn into brown raisins.

Frank's Bike Ride

Frank has moved to a new town. He does not know his way around very well. Today he went for a bike ride to explore the area. He didn't note all the turns he made. Now Frank is lost!

2. Which sentence tells what most likely happens next?
   - ○ A. Frank will fall off his bike.
   - ○ B. Frank will ask for directions.
   - ○ C. Frank will explore more.

To parents   Go to page 77 and do Activity 3 or 4 with your child.

Exercise 16

Read the paragraph. Then fill in the bubble that best answers each question.

The Snowshoe Hare

Each summer the snowshoe hare's fur is brown. It is hard for enemies to see the hare on the brown land of the Arctic. But winter is coming. It will soon snow. The hare's thick fur will change color to help keep it safe.

1. Which sentence tells what most likely happens next?
   - ○ A. The hare's coat will become white.
   - ○ B. The hare's enemies will see it in the snow.
   - ○ C. The Arctic snow will turn brown.

The Spelling Bee

The spelling bee was almost over. Only Peggy and Tony were left. Tony spelled M-A-G-A-Z-I-N-E correctly. Then it was Peggy's turn. The word was S-I-T-U-A-T-I-O-N. Peggy did not know how to spell it. Tony did.

2. Which sentence tells what most likely happens next?
   - ○ A. Peggy will win.
   - ○ B. Tony will help Peggy.
   - ○ C. Tony will win.

To parents   Go to page 77 and do Activity 3 or 4 with your child.

Exercise 17

Read the paragraph. Then fill in the bubble that best answers each question.

Juan and the Watch

Juan found a watch in front of a neighbor's apartment. He took the watch to the neighbors. They were very grateful to get their watch. They gave Juan a reward.

1. Which sentence tells what most likely happens next?
   - ○ A. Juan will look for other watches.
   - ○ B. Juan will thank them.
   - ○ C. Juan will ask for food.

Jean's Role

Jean has a role in the class play. She didn't learn her lines well. She didn't pay attention at rehearsals. Today is the big performance. Everyone's parents are coming.

2. Which sentence tells what most likely happens next?
   - ○ A. Jean will forget her lines.
   - ○ B. Jean will get the most applause.
   - ○ C. Jean's parents will be proud.

To parents Go to page 77 and do Activity 3 or 4 with your child.

Date: _____

Exercise 18

Read the paragraph. Then fill in the bubble that best answers each question.

Garden Melons

Jon planted some pumpkins in his garden. He watered the plants as they grew. He pulled out weeds so the plants had plenty of room. Now the pumpkins are almost ripe.

1. Which sentence tells what most likely happens next?
   - ○ A. Jon will pick the pumpkins.
   - ○ B. Jon will cut the leaves off.
   - ○ C. Jon will go away.

The Race

Deedee is planning to run in a race this weekend. She has been working out for weeks to get ready. Today she slipped on a wet sidewalk. Now her ankle hurts. She can't put any weight on it.

2. Which sentence tells what most likely happens next?
   - ○ A. Deedee will drop out of the race.
   - ○ B. Someone will run for Deedee.
   - ○ C. Deedee will run in the race anyway.

To parents Go to page 77 and do Activity 3 or 4 with your child.

Exercise 19

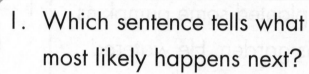

Read the paragraph. Then fill in the bubble that best answers each question.

A Family Picnic

The Alanos went on a family picnic. They chose a pretty place to sit. It had a nice view of a pond. No one saw the anthill. They spread a blanket and took out the food from the basket. The family began to eat.

1. Which sentence tells what most likely happens next?
   - ○ A. Mr Alano will fall in the pond.
   - ○ B. Mrs Alano will sleep.
   - ○ C. The ants will share the picnic.

Tessa's Room

Tessa has a messy room. Her books, games and clothes are scattered all over. Tomorrow Tessa's grandmother is coming for a visit. Tessa's dad has come up to her room for a talk.

2. Which sentence tells what most likely happens next?
   - ○ A. Tessa's dad will clean up the room.
   - ○ B. Tessa's grandmother will visit another time.
   - ○ C. Tessa's dad will tell Tessa to clean her room.

To parents Go to page 77 and do Activity 3 or 4 with your child.

Exercise 20

Read the paragraph. Then fill in the bubble that best answers each question.

Boxer

Boxer was getting restless. His owner wasn't at home to play fetch with him. Then he saw Spiky in the neighbor's garden. Spiky is the cat from next door. He loves chasing Spiky. Boxer started to run.

1. Which sentence tells what most likely happens next?
   - ○ A. Boxer will chase Spiky.
   - ○ B. Boxer will run home.
   - ○ C. Spiky will chase Boxer.

A Colorful Story

The old lady looked at the painting in the building. It looked very faded. So, she wanted to help the owners repaint the picture. She took out her box of paints and started work. Oh no! She can't paint very well.

2. Which sentence tells what most likely happens next?
   - ○ A. The painting will look ugly.
   - ○ B. The old lady will give up.
   - ○ C. The old lady will throw the painting away.

To parents   Go to page 77 and do Activity 3 or 4 with your child.

Identifying Fact and Opinion

Being able to identify and distinguish between a fact and an opinion is an important reading comprehension skill, especially as readers start to encounter a variety of texts. A reader who can differentiate between statements of fact and opinion are better able to analyze and assess a text. The passages and questions in this section will help your child learn to identify statements of fact and opinion.

This section will provide opportunities for your child to understand that a fact can be proved to be true, while an opinion is what someone thinks or believes and is a kind of judgment.

The extension activities provide additional challenges to your child to encourage and develop her understanding of the particular comprehension skill.

Exercise 1

Read the paragraph. Then follow the instructions.

The Dangers of Using a Cellphone

Many countries have banned cellphone
use in the car. It is very dangerous.
A cellphone can distract drivers. In countries
like Australia, France and Greece, the
use of cellphones in cars has been banned.
A heavy fine should be imposed on those who ignore this ban.
Countries all over the world should follow this ban.

1. Write *fact* or *opinion* next to each sentence.

    _____ A. A cellphone can distract drivers.

    _____ B. In countries like Australia, France and Greece,
       the use of cellphones in cars has been banned.

    _____ C. Countries all over the world should follow
       this ban.

2. Write another opinion from the paragraph.

    _____

    _____

To parents   Go to page 78 and do Activity 5 or 6 with your child.

Date: _____

Exercise 2

Read the paragraph. Then follow the instructions.

The Hibiscus

The hibiscus is a beautiful flower. It
comes in different colors of red, yellow,
and orange. In parts of Asia, the most
common color for the hibiscus is red. In
some countries like South Korea and Malaysia, it is also a national
flower. The hibiscus flower can be dried and made into tea. It tastes
delicious. However, some people don't like it as much as others.

1. Write *fact* or *opinion* next to each sentence.

    _____ A. In some countries like South Korea and
    Malaysia, it is also a national flower.

    _____ B. The hibiscus is a beautiful flower.

    _____ C. The hibiscus flower can be dried and made
    into tea.

2. Write another fact from the paragraph.

    _____

    _____

    _____

To parents Go to page 78 and do Activity 5 or 6 with your child.

58

Exercise 3

Read the paragraph. Then follow the instructions.

The Land Down Under

Sydney, Australia is a great place to live.
The weather is temperate. Sydney has
four seasons in a year. They are summer,
autumn, winter, and spring. Throughout
all four seasons, most people who live
in Sydney go to the beach. They enjoy doing beach activities
including swimming. They must lead such a nice life.

1. Write *fact* or *opinion* next to each sentence.
   _____ A. Sydney has four seasons in a year.
   _____ B. Sydney, Australia is a great place to live.
   _____ C. Throughout all four seasons, most people who
   live in Sydney go to the beach.

2. Write another opinion from the paragraph.

   _____

   _____

   _____

To parents Go to page 78 and do Activity 5 or 6 with your child.

Date: _____

Exercise 4

Read the paragraph. Then follow the instructions.

Ghiradelli Chocolates

Ghiradelli Chocolates was started by
an Italian man named Ghiradelli. His
chocolates are made in San Francisco.
They are some of the best chocolates in
America. People who visit San Francisco
should visit his chocolate shop. It can be a great tourist attraction.
His shop sells chocolate biscuits, cakes, milkshakes and sundaes.

1. Write *fact* or *opinion* next to each sentence.

   _____ A. Ghiradelli Chocolates was started by an
   Italian man named Ghiradelli.

   _____ B. It can be a great tourist attraction.

   _____ C. His chocolates are made in San Francisco.

2. Write another fact from the paragraph.

   _____

   _____

   _____

To parents   Go to page 78 and do Activity 5 or 6 with your child.

Exercise 5

Read the paragraph. Then follow the instructions.

Hospitals

Hospitals are important buildings. They provide medical care for those who are ill. Every hospital has an emergency unit. There are doctors at the emergency unit to treat sick people. Emergency units should  have many doctors. This ensures that everybody gets the attention they need. Every town should have a hospital nearby.

1. Write *fact* or *opinion* next to each sentence.

    _____ A. There are doctors at the emergency unit to treat sick people.

    _____ B. Emergency units should have many doctors.

    _____ C. They provide medical care for those who are ill.

2. Write another opinion from the paragraph.

    _____

    _____

    _____

To parents   Go to page 78 and do Activity 5 or 6 with your child.

61

Date: _____

Exercise 6

Read the paragraph. Then follow the instructions.

A Famous Fast Food Chain

McDonald's is a famous fast food chain. It can be found in most parts of the world. It is recognizable through the big yellow arch or 'M'. In Australia, McDonald's is called Mackers for short. McDonald serves yummy food. It serves burgers, fries, cakes and drinks. It should be visited at least once a week.

1. Write *fact* or *opinion* next to each sentence.

    _____ A. It is recognizable through the big yellow arch or 'M'.

    _____ B. McDonald serves yummy food.

    _____ C. In Australia, McDonald's is called Mackers for short.

2. Write another opinion from the paragraph.

    _____

    _____

    _____

To parents   Go to page 78 and do Activity 5 or 6 with your child.

Exercise 7

Read the paragraph. Then follow the instructions.

Wonderful Nike Shoes

Nike is a very popular shoe brand. You can identify Nike shoes through its white tick. Nike's tag line is 'Just Do It'. It tells athletes to be the best they can be. Nike shoes are comfortable and safe for the feet. They are good for people who are training for track activities or simply jogging. Everyone should own a pair of Nike shoes.

1. Write *fact* or *opinion* next to each sentence.

    _____ A. You can identify Nike shoes through its white tick.

    _____ B. Nike shoes are comfortable and safe for the feet.

    _____ C. Nike's tag line is 'Just Do It'.

2. Write another fact from the paragraph.

    _____

    _____

    _____

To parents   Go to page 78 and do Activity 5 or 6 with your child.

Exercise 8

Read the paragraph. Then follow the instructions.

Purchasing a Good Computer

When we buy a new computer, we look for a brand we can trust. Dell computers is a good computer brand. Dell's brand name is in blue. It is easily recognizable. Its products are not expensive. Students should be able to afford Dell computers. If people want to own a computer, they should get a Dell.

1. Write *fact* or *opinion* next to each sentence.

   _____ A. Dell computers is a good computer brand.

   _____ B. Its products are not expensive.

   _____ C. If people want to own a computer, they should get a Dell.

2. Write another fact from the paragraph.

   _____

   _____

   _____

To parents   Go to page 78 and do Activity 5 or 6 with your child.

Exercise 9

Read the paragraph. Then follow the instructions.

Educational Programs

There are many educational programs for children. Some examples include 'Bananas in Pajamas', 'Thomas the Tank Engine' or 'Barney and Friends'. These programs teach young children about language, counting, good manners and other things. They include cute characters and a lot of songs. They are great for children. Parents should encourage their children to watch these programs.

1. Write *fact* or *opinion* next to each sentence.

   _____ A. There are many educational programs for children.

   _____ B. They include cute characters and a lot of songs.

   _____ C. They are great for children.

2. Write another opinion from the paragraph.

   _____

   _____

   _____

To parents Go to page 78 and do Activity 5 or 6 with your child.

Exercise 10

Read the paragraph. Then follow the instructions.

The Rainbow

A rainbow sometimes appears after it
rains. There are seven primary colors
in the rainbow. They are red, orange,
yellow, green, blue, indigo and violet.
This is a beautiful combination of colors. Many people enjoy
looking out for rainbows. Seeing a rainbow can make you feel
happy inside.

1. Write *fact* or *opinion* next to each sentence.
   - _____ A. There are seven primary colors in the rainbow.
   - _____ B. This is a beautiful combination of colors.
   - _____ C. They are red, orange, yellow, green, blue,
     indigo and violet.

2. Write another fact from the paragraph.
   _____

   _____

   _____

To parents   Go to page 78 and do Activity 5 or 6 with your child.

Date: _____

Exercise 11

Read the paragraph. Then follow the instructions.

The Pyramids

The pyramids at Giza are considered one of the wonders of the world. The Great Pyramid of Cheops is the biggest pyramid in the world. It stands at 137 meters high. It is made from over 2 million giant stone blocks. It is a magnificent structure. The pyramids are a great tourist attraction. Everybody should visit the pyramids.

1. Write *fact* or *opinion* next to each sentence.

   _____ A. The pyramids are a great tourist attraction.

   _____ B. The pyramids at Giza are considered one of the wonders of the world.

   _____ C. The Great Pyramid of Cheops is the biggest pyramid in the world.

2. Write another opinion from the paragraph.

   _____

   _____

   _____

To parents Go to page 78 and do Activity 5 or 6 with your child.

67

Exercise 12

Read the paragraph. Then follow the instructions.

The Victoria Falls

Victoria Falls can be seen from either
Zimbabwe or Zambia. The falls were
named after Queen Victoria. It stretches
for 1.7 kilometers and is 100 meters
deep. Tourists should spend a couple of hours exploring the falls.
The experience of being sprayed by the falls is an interesting one.

1. Write *fact* or *opinion* next to each sentence.

   _____ A. Tourists should spend a couple of hours
   exploring the falls.

   _____ B. The falls were named after Queen Victoria.

   _____ C. It stretches for 1.7 kilometers and is 100
   meters deep.

2. Write another fact from the paragraph.

   _____

   _____

   _____

To parents   Go to page 78 and do Activity 5 or 6 with your child.

Date: _____

Exercise 13

Read the paragraph. Then follow the instructions.

Volcanos

Volcanos are an opening in the planet's
surface. Mount Etna in Sicily, Italy is a
famous volcano. Its last eruption was in
March 2012. Volcanic eruptions can
be dangerous. The ash and gas that comes out of volcanoes can
kill people. Volcanos can be interesting too. Schools should take
students to visit dormant volcanos.

1. Write *fact* or *opinion* next to each sentence.

    _____ A. Mount Etna in Sicily, Italy is a famous volcano.

    _____ B. The ash and gas that comes out of volcanoes
    can kill people.

    _____ C. Volcanoes can be interesting too.

2. Write another opinion from the paragraph.

    _____

    _____

    _____

To parents Go to page 78 and do Activity 5 or 6 with your child.

69

Exercise 14

Read the paragraph. Then follow the instructions.

Football

Football is a sport played by many countries around the world. The aim of the game is to score a goal into the opponent's goal. A football team can

consist of 11 to 18 players. It is a game that is played between two teams. Football is also known as soccer. It is a highly enjoyable game. Playing football is one of the best forms of exercise.

1. Write *fact* or *opinion* next to each sentence.
   _____ A. A football team can consist of 11 to 18 players.
   _____ B. It is a highly enjoyable game.
   _____ C. The aim of the game is to score a goal into the opponent's goal.

2. Write another opinion from the paragraph.

   _____

   _____

   _____

To parents   Go to page 78 and do Activity 5 or 6 with your child.

Exercise 15

Read the paragraph. Then follow the instructions.

The Calendar

A calendar helps organize days in a year
The English word *calendar* comes from
the Latin word *kalendae*. There are many
types of calendars. The calendar often
used today is the Gregorian calendar.
Calendars are important for everyone. One should be taught
how to read and use the calendar at an early age.

1. Write *fact* or *opinion* next to each sentence.

   _____ A. The English word *calendar* comes from the
   Latin word *kalendae*.

   _____ B. One should be taught to how to read and use
   the calendar at an early age.

   _____ C. A calendar helps organize days in a year.

2. Write another opinion from the paragraph.

   _____

   _____

   _____

To parents   Go to page 78 and do Activity 5 or 6 with your child.

Exercise 16

Read the paragraph. Then follow the instructions.

A Golden Retriever

Dogs are man's best friend. A good dog to have is a golden retriever. Golden retrievers originate from Scotland. They make good guide dogs for the blind. They are sometimes used as hearing dogs for the deaf. Golden retrievers are friendly. They are good dogs to have around children.

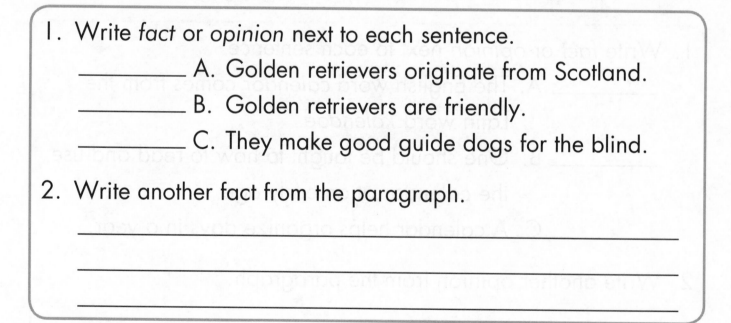

1. Write *fact* or *opinion* next to each sentence.

   _____ A. Golden retrievers originate from Scotland.

   _____ B. Golden retrievers are friendly.

   _____ C. They make good guide dogs for the blind.

2. Write another fact from the paragraph.

   _____

   _____

   _____

To parents Go to page 78 and do Activity 5 or 6 with your child.

Exercise 17

Read the paragraph. Then follow the instructions.

Swimming

Swimming is a popular sport. It has
become a great recreational and sporting
activity. For some people, it is a form
of daily exercise. In some countries,

swimming has become part of the education curriculum. Swimming
is also a sport in the Olympics. All children should be taught how to
swim at an early age.

1. Write *fact* or *opinion* next to each sentence.

    _____ A. In some countries, swimming has become part
                 of the education curriculum.

    _____ B. Swimming is also a sport in the Olympics.

    _____ C. All children should be taught how to swim at
                 an early age.

2. Write another opinion from the paragraph.

_____

_____

_____

To parents   Go to page 78 and do Activity 5 or 6 with your child.

Date: _____

Exercise 18

Read the paragraph. Then follow the instructions.

The Beauty of a Horse

Horses are beautiful, spirited animals.
A female horse is called a mare. A young
horse is called a foal. Horses live between
25 to 30 years. Horses are used in
activities such as police work, entertainment and therapy. Horses are
good for young children. They are a comfort to the lost and lonely.

1. Write *fact* or *opinion* next to each sentence.
   - _____ A. A female horse is called a mare.
   - _____ B. A young horse is called a foal.
   - _____ C. They are a comfort to the lost and lonely.

2. Write another fact from the paragraph.

   _____

   _____

   _____

To parents   Go to page 78 and do Activity 5 or 6 with your child.

Date: _____

Exercise 19

Read the paragraph. Then follow the instructions.

A Living Saint

Mother Theresa of Calcutta was called
a living saint. She took care of the poor
and sickly people in India. She founded
the Missionaries of Charity in 1950. She
received the Nobel Prize in 1979. No one deserved the prize more
than Mother Theresa. She will forever be in the hearts of people.

1. Write *fact* or *opinion* next to each sentence.

   _____ A. She founded the Missionaries of Charity
   in 1950.

   _____ B. She received the Nobel Prize in 1979.

   _____ C. She will forever be in the hearts of people.

2. Write another opinion from the paragraph.

   _____

   _____

   _____

To parents   Go to page 78 and do Activity 5 or 6 with your child.

Exercise 20

Read the paragraph. Then follow the instructions.

The Importance of Recycling

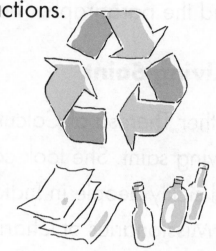

Recycling is a habit that should be practiced regularly. The average American uses about 650 pounds of paper each year. Americans use about 2.5 million plastic bottles every hour. Such actions are hurting our environment. Everybody should reduce, reuse and recycle.

1. Write *fact* or *opinion* next to each sentence.

    _____ A. The average American uses about 650 pounds of paper each year.

    _____ B. Such actions are hurting our environment.

    _____ C. Americans use about 2.5 million plastic bottles every hour.

2. Write another opinion from the paragraph.

    _____

    _____

    _____

To parents Go to page 78 and do Activity 5 or 6 with your child.

Extension Activities

Activity 1: Organizing ideas

Skill: Identifying main idea and details

Read the text again with your child. Get
you child to highlight the main idea.
Then get your child to identify the details
that support the main idea. Finally, get
your child to list the main idea and the
supporting details in a graphic organizer like the one here.

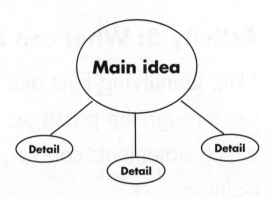

Activity 2: Text Scramble

Skill: Identifying main idea and details

Choose two passages from pages 7 to 34. Write each sentence
of the passages on strips of paper and mix up the strips. Then
challenge your child to organize the strips starting with the main
idea of each text and then the supporting details for each.

Activity 3: What do you think will happen?

Skill: Making predictions

Use short stories (especially those with artwork) to help your child
make predictions. Start reading the story to your child. Before
turning each page, ask your child to guess what might happen next
in the story. Then, get your child to say why she thinks so. You may
want to provide hints to guide your child.

Activity 4: What's in a title?

Skill: Making predictions

Choose some headlines from magazines or newspapers that are suitable for your child. Challenge your child to think about what the article could be about based on the title of the article.

Activity 5: What can be proven?

Skill: Identifying Fact and Opinion

Go through the passages with your child. Ask your child to say which statements can be proven and which are the writer's opinion.

Activity 6: Kinds of Statements

Skill: Identifying Fact and Opinion

Go through different kinds of text with your child. Show him advertisements and newspaper articles. Show how there are more facts in newspaper articles compared to advertisements.

Answer Key

Page 7	**Page 21**	**Page 36**
1. C 2. C	1. A 2. A	1. B 2. B
Page 8	**Page 22**	**Page 37**
1. C 2. C	1. A 2. A	1. A 2. A
Page 9	**Page 23**	**Page 38**
1. B 2. A	1. A 2. B	1. C 2. B
Page 10	**Page 24**	**Page 39**
1. C 2. A	1. A 2. B	1. B 2. A
Page 11	**Page 25**	**Page 40**
1. B 2. B	1. A 2. A	1. A 2. A
Page 12	**Page 26**	**Page 41**
1. C 2. C	1. B 2. A	1. B 2. B
Page 13	**Page 27**	**Page 42**
1. A 2. A	1. A 2. A	1. A 2. B
Page 14	**Page 28**	**Page 43**
1. B 2. C	1. A 2. B	1. C 2. C
Page 15	**Page 29**	**Page 44**
1. A 2. B	1. C 2. C	1. B 2. C
Page 16	**Page 30**	**Page 45**
1. C 2. A	1. A 2. A	1. B 2. B
Page 17	**Page 31**	**Page 46**
1. A 2. A	1. C 2. C	1. B 2. B
Page 18	**Page 32**	**Page 47**
1. A 2. A	1. C 2. B	1. A 2. A
Page 19	**Page 33**	**Page 48**
1. A 2. A	1. A 2. A	1. C 2. A
Page 20	**Page 34**	**Page 49**
1. C 2. C	1. A 2. C	1. B 2. A

Page 50

1. C   2. B

Page 51

1. A   2. C

Page 52

1. B   2. A

Page 53

1. A   2. A

Page 54

1. C   2. C

Page 55

1. A   2. A

Page 57

1. A. Fact   B. Fact   C. Opinion
2. It is very dangerous. / A heavy fine should be imposed on those who ignore this ban.

Page 58

1. A. Fact   B. Opinion   C. Fact
B. It comes in different colors of red, yellow, and orange. / In parts of Asia, the most common color for the hibiscus is red.

Page 59

1. A. Fact   B. Opinion   C. Fact
2. They must lead such a nice life.

Page 60

1. A. Fact   B. Opinion   C. Fact
2. His shop sells chocolate biscuits, cakes, milkshakes and sundaes.

Page 61

1. A. Fact   B. Opinion   C. Fact
2. Hospitals are important buildings. / Every town should have a hospital nearby.

Page 62

1. A. Fact   B. Opinion   C. Fact
2. It should be visited at least once a week.

Page 63

1. A. Fact   B. Opinion   C. Fact
2. It tells athletes to be the best they can be.

Page 64

1. A. Opinion   B. Opinion   C. Opinion
2. When we buy a new computer, we look for a brand name we can trust. / Dell's brand name is in blue.

Page 65

1. A. Fact   B. Opinion   C. Opinion
2. Parents should encourage their children to watch these programs.

Page 66

1. A. Fact   B. Opinion   C. Fact
2. A rainbow sometimes appears after it rains.

Page 67

1. A. Opinion   B. Fact   C. Fact
2. It is a magnificent structure. / Everybody should visit the pyramids.

Page 68

1. A. Opinion   B. Fact   C. Fact
2. Victoria Falls can be seen from either Zimbabwe or Zambia.

Page 69

1. A. Fact   B. Fact   C. Opinion
2. Volcanos can be interesting too. / Schools should take students to visit dormant volcanos.

Page 70

1. A. Fact   B. Opinion   C. Fact
2. Playing football is one of the best forms of exercise.

Page 71

1. A. Fact   B. Opinion   C. Fact
2. Calendars are important for everyone.

Page 72

1. A. Fact   B. Opinion   C. Opinion
2. They are sometimes used as hearing dogs for the deaf.

Page 73

1. A. Fact   B. Fact   C. Opinion
2. It has become a great recreational and sporting activity.

Page 74

1. A. Fact   B. Fact   C. Opinion
2. Horses live between 25 to 30 years. / Horses are used in activities such as police work, entertainment and therapy.

Page 75

1. A. Fact   B. Fact   C. Opinion
2. No one deserved the prize more than Mother Theresa.

Page 76

1. A. Fact   B. Opinion   C. Fact
2. Recycling is a habit that should be practiced regularly. / Everybody should reduce, reuse and recycle.